To the Kraut and Zonderman families
—K.T.

Historical photos used in collage artworks throughout the book are courtesy of the Library of Congress.
Additional photo on page 30 courtesy of YIVO Encyclopedia/Wikimedia Commons.
Recording by klezmer musician Yale Strom, edited for us from a concert at Eldridge Street Synagogue

KAR-BEN PUBLISHING®
An imprint of Lerner Publishing Group, Inc.
241 First Avenue North
Minneapolis, MN 55401 USA

Website address: www.karben.com

Main body text set in Fontoon ITC Std.
Typeface provided by International Typeface Corp.

Library of Congress Cataloging-in-Publication Data

Names: Teis, Kyra, author, illustrator.
Title: Klezmer! / Kyra Teis.
Description: Minneapolis : Kar-Ben Publishing ®, 2021. | Audience: Ages 4–8 | Audience: Grades K–1 | Summary: "A child makes a music-filled visit to her grandparents' apartment on the Lower East Side. Along the way, she dances to klezmer music, connecting its Old Country beginnings to its new rockin' vibe"— Provided by publisher.
Identifiers: LCCN 2020040548 (print) | LCCN 2020040549 (ebook) | ISBN 9781541598003 (trade hardcover) | ISBN 9781541598010 (paperback) | ISBN 9781728428932 (ebook)
Subjects: LCSH: Klezmer music—History and criticism—Juvenile literature. | CYAC: Klezmer music—History and criticism.
Classification: LCC ML3776 .T45 2021 (print) | LCC ML3776 (ebook) | DDC 781.62/924—dc23

LC record available at https://lccn.loc.gov/2020040548
LC ebook record available at https://lccn.loc.gov/2020040549

Manufactured in the United States of America
1-47992-48670-11/10/2020

Klezmer!

by Kyra Teis

KAR-BEN
PUBLISHING

Klezmer's cool vibe
is like taking a ride
to a jam session
in the city.

Klezmer's
family and friends,
clarinet and violin,

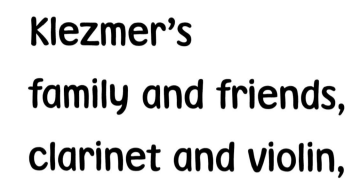

from Uptown,
Downtown, and
Lower East Side.

Klezmer pulls
out a chair
and invites you
to share

a little nosh,
a good joke.

The fiddle sighs,
"Ahhhh, the good old days,"
playing a memory
across its strings.

OY!

Let's rock out, already!

Stir in some bass—

BOWM

BOWM!

set the pace.

A dash of accordion.

Turn up the heat!
Clarinet squawks and bleats.

A recipe of sound.
Flavors from the Old Country,
seasoned with the here-and-now,

a drain-the-bowl,
touch-the-soul
groove.

Klezmer's oldish, and newish,
like jazz, but it's Jewish.
Yesteryear's hits
strive
to jive

with new riffs.

Music bold and loud,
rhythms wild and proud,
frenzied,
electric,
always eclectic,
moving the crowd
to a 2/2 metric.

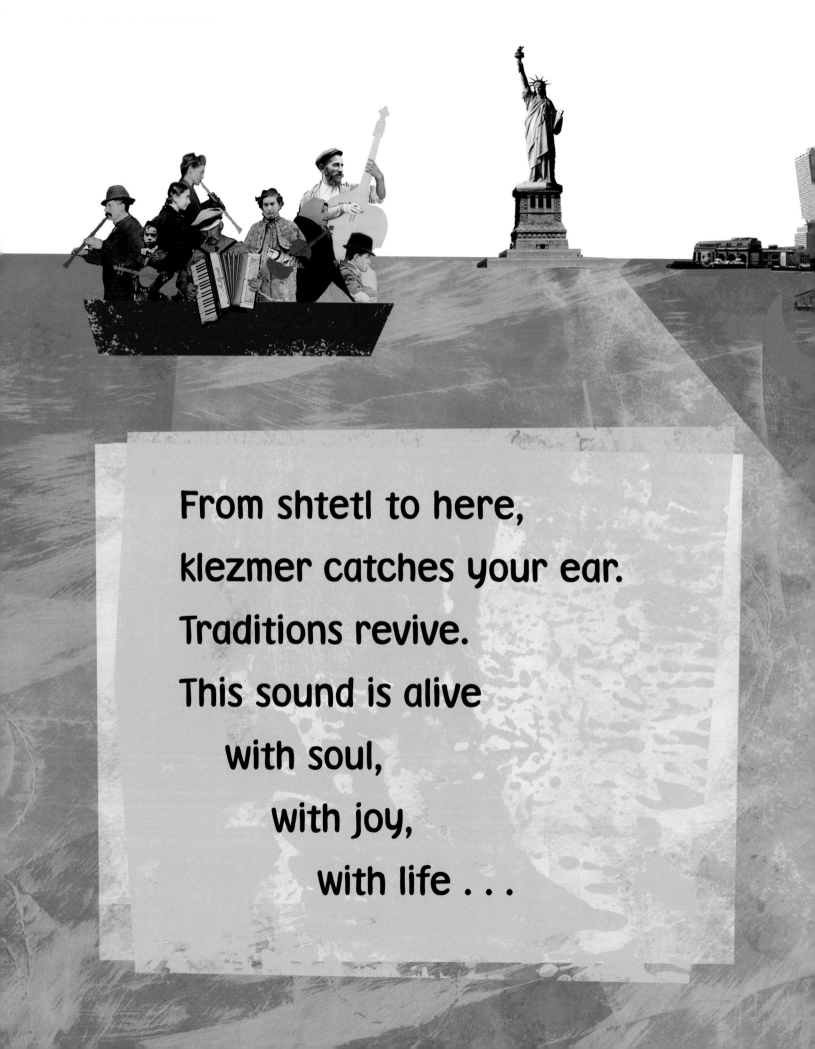

From shtetl to here,

klezmer catches your ear.

Traditions revive.

This sound is alive

with soul,

with joy,

with life . . .

To klezmer!

About Klezmer Music

In the late 1800s and early 1900s, there was a wave of Jewish immigration from Russia and Poland to New York's Lower East Side. These immigrants brought their music with them, playing it at weddings and other celebrations. These new Americans wanted to blend in, rather than keep up their old musical traditions, so they remixed what they called Jewish music to reflect American tastes like Dixieland and big band swing.

The music as it was played originally all but died out, but the 1970s brought a revival of interest in Jewish music from eastern Europe. Young musicians, curious about the music of their parents and grandparents and wanting to study the unique sound, sought out old-timers. This music became known as klezmer music after the traveling musicians called klezmorim. Klezmer music, once a dying tradition, now enjoys large and appreciative audiences all over the world.

Scan the QR code
to watch a modern performance
of klezmer music!

Kyra Teis is a children's book author-illustrator, a graphic novelist, and an avid sewer of costumes. When she's not making art, you can find her, cheering wildly with her husband, at their two daughters' soccer games and musical theater productions.